Ft. Lauderdale

GAYCATION 2

William Giancursio

For
Tommy P
Thanks for all the fun, laughs,
and
miles of smiles.

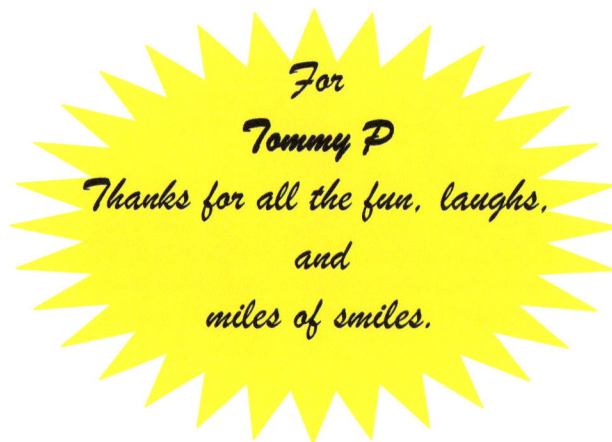

ISBN: 978-0-578-06535-9

Gaycation 2

Way back in 1990, I borrowed my friend Joe's SLR camera and snapped a roll of film to use as reference material for an oil painting that I wanted to do, entitled "Friends of Dorothy." For the past 20 years, I have taken quite a few photographs for oil paintings, watercolors, drawings, sculptures, and photo books. They all have one thing in common, action figures. The fascination I developed playing with these miniature mannequins has grown and evolved over the years. What began as reference material for paintings and drawings has developed into a photographic exploration that I find unique and gratifying.

My original intent was to create a series of artworks that made statements about gay culture. Everything I photographed was constructed in small scale, proportionate to the action figures. As time went by, the staging for the photos became more and more complex. I spent days, weeks, and months building intricate small sets and props to mimic the real world. Then one day, while vacationing in Ft. Lauderdale, I began photographing the action figures in real life environments using distance to simulate the scale of the figures and with the aid of a very few small-scale props. The gap was bridged between the real and the imaginary. The action figures moved from their world to ours. That exploration resulted in Ft. Lauderdale Gaycation, my fourth book.

The eye of the camera impressed me with how well it could fool my eye into believing a different kind of reality. It was a brilliant moment of discovery, although I am not, by any means, a genius. What I am is creative. Somewhere in my notes I have copied the phrase, "Creative people alter the frame of reference through which we see the world around us." What this says to me is that creative people not only present us with different ways of seeing, but they also present us with different ways of thinking. For some people, art will only be something mindless and pretty, something one hangs on a wall to compliment one's sofa and draperies. For me, nothing could be further from the truth. Good art is and will always be engaging and confrontational. Without these ingredients, there is no challenge to the mind. Without challenge there is no impetus to grow. While art that is pretty to look at may be interesting, art that allows us to think defines our sense of who we are.

This past winter, while once again vacationing in Florida, I shot a sequel to Ft. Lauderdale Gaycation. This sequel is much more premeditated than its predecessor. This time, I brought along quite a few props, a dozen action figures, and their impressive wardrobes. I took photos of the "boys" all over Ft. Lauderdale. They went back to the beach, had a cook-out, and attended a private party. I even treated them to a delicious dinner at a fine restaurant, complete with entertaining drag queens. And what would a vacation be without a shopping spree at the stores along Las Olas Blvd?

I have become very accustomed to my yearly visits to sunny locales. I would highly recommend a warm vacation to anyone who struggles to get through a long, dreary, northern winter. If you should be lucky enough to get away, and if by chance you encounter a man moving at the speed of light with a camera and an arm full of action figures, it's probably just me, working on another book.

So put on your swimsuit, grab a towel and your flip-flops, and above all, don't forget the sunscreen. It's time to return to Ft. Lauderdale, for Gaycation 2.

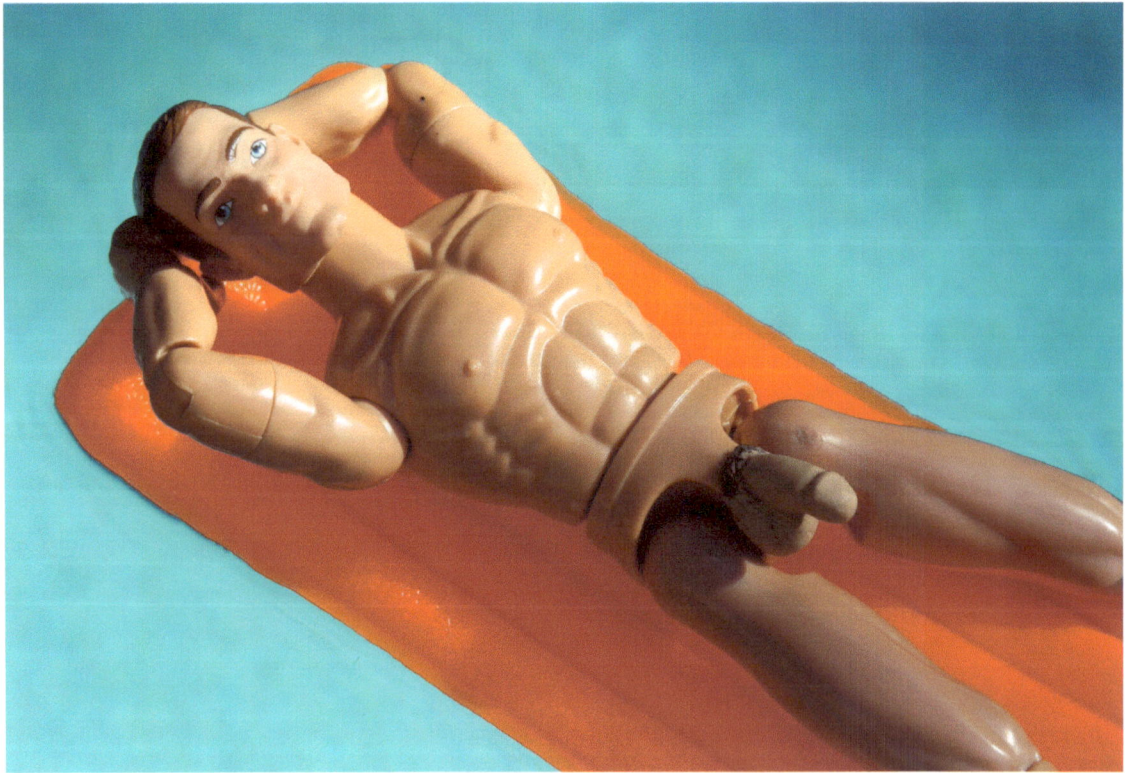

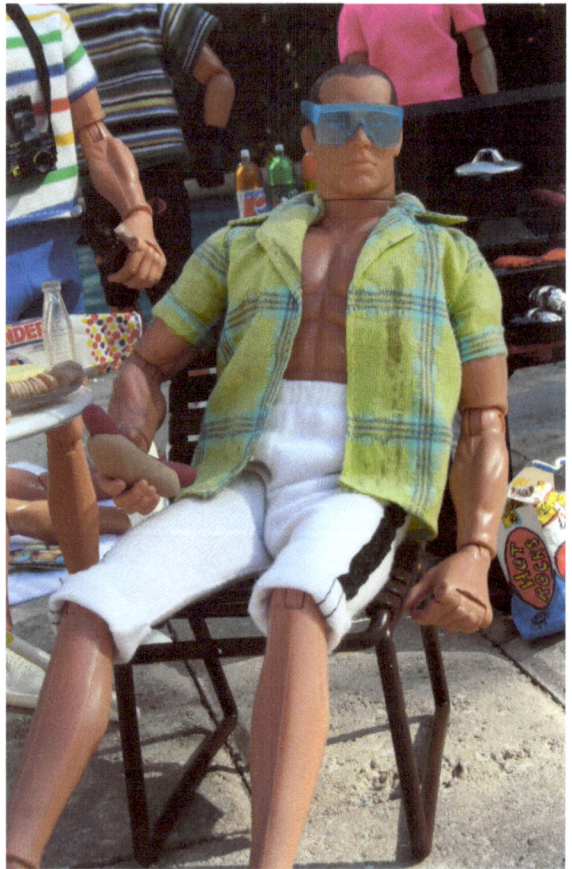

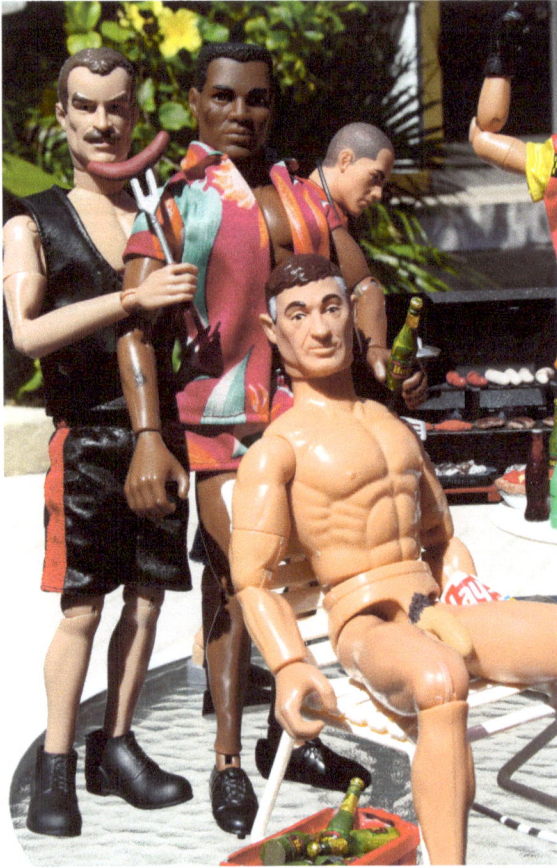

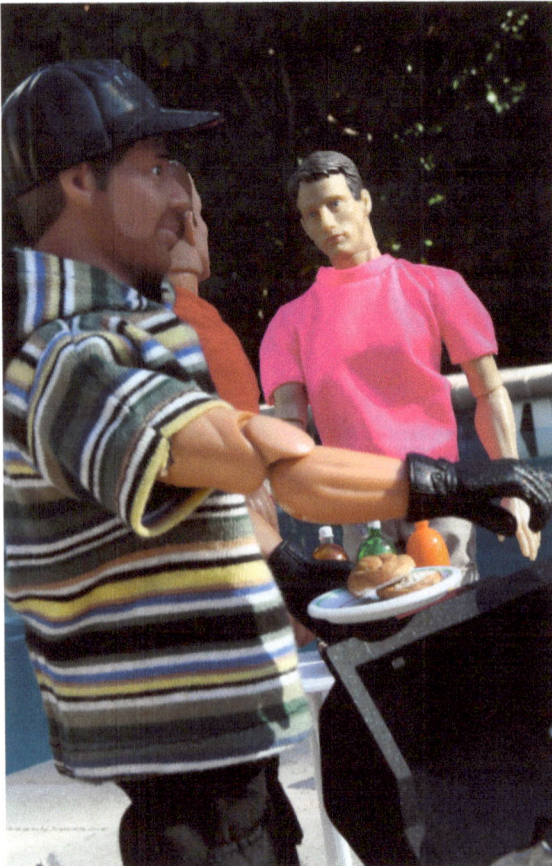

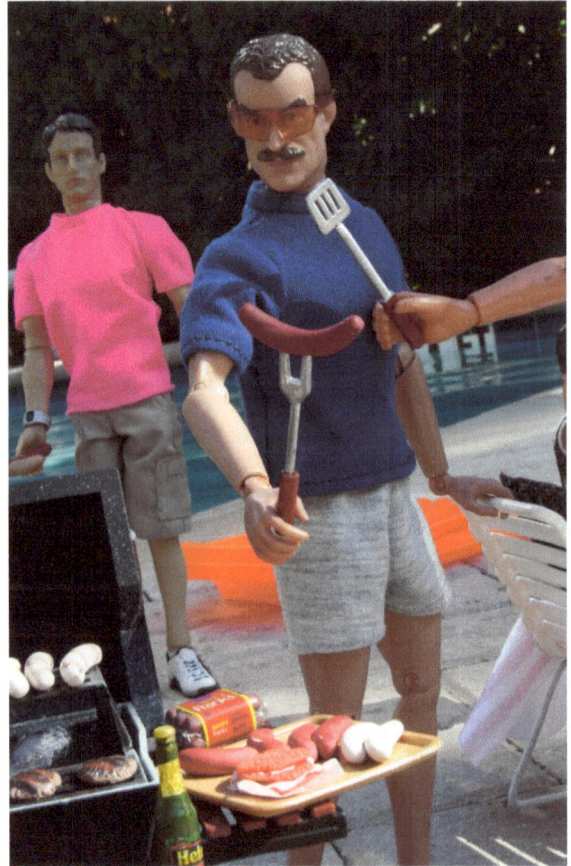